Forty Days with Jesus

By Clay Gentry

Published by
Spiritbuilding Publishers
9700 Ferry Road, Waynesville, Ohio 45068

FORTY DAYS WITH JESUS
By Clay Gentry

ISBN: 978–1–964–80516–0

Spiritbuilding
PUBLISHERS

spiritbuilding.com

Table of Contents

Special Thanks to …

… The saints at the Jackson Heights church of Christ
for their gracious love that enables me to preach and teach
the gospel of Jesus Christ.

… My wife Shelly for her love and support.
Without you by my side this trip through life
would not be possible.

A Note from Clay

Imagine a journey of transformation, a period of profound spiritual growth that unfolds in just 40 days. Throughout history, the number 40 has held a special significance in the realm of spiritual preparation.

When the rains fell for 40 days and nights, Noah's world was cleansed, making way for a new beginning. Moses, after 40 days on the solitary heights of Mount Sinai, descended with the tablets of the law, forever changed by his encounter with God. Even Jesus, before embarking on His public ministry, spent 40 days in the wilderness, preparing for the work ahead. Time and again, we see this number appear in Scripture:

- Noah's life and the world were transformed by 40 days of rain (Genesis 7:1–24).
- Moses was a different man after spending 40 days on Mount Sinai with God (Exodus 24:15–18).
- The Israelite spies scouted the Promised Land for 40 days (Numbers 13:1–33).
- Goliath spent 40 days challenging the Israelite army while God prepared David to confront him (1 Samuel 17:1–54).
- Elijah ran more than two hundred miles in 40 days on one meal to get to a place where he could hear from God again (1 Kings 19:1–18).
- The people of Nineveh were transformed in 40 days after God's challenge to change their ways (Jonah 3:1–10).
- Jesus was empowered for ministry by spending 40 days in the desert (Mark 1:12–13).
- The disciples were transformed by spending 40 days with the resurrected Jesus (Acts 1:1–4).

Just as God used 40 days to prepare these individuals for His purposes, He desires to do the same for you today. This 40-day journey with Jesus is an invitation to encounter Him in a deeper way, to experience His transforming power in your own life.

This study is designed with five readings per week, allowing you flexibility as you walk with Jesus. If you miss a day, simply pick it up the next. Commit to this journey, and over the next 40 days, you'll discover a deeper intimacy with Jesus, a renewed sense of purpose, and a greater understanding of His love for you.

If this study is helping you, or if you have spiritual questions. I'd love to hear from you. Drop me a line at *clay@thebibleway.org*. Or if you're ever in the Columbia, Tennessee, area let's grab a cup of coffee and talk about our Savior (and maybe a little Elvis, too!).

Introduction to Mark

Coming in at just 661 verses, Mark is the shortest of the four gospels. Still, his fast-paced and vivid account of the life of Jesus makes it the perfect introduction to "Jesus Christ, the Son of God" (1:1).

AUTHOR

Unlike the epistles, the gospel writers never identified themselves (ref. Romans 1:1; et. al). However, widespread evidence from early church writings affirms that John Mark wrote the second gospel. Mark is a recurring character throughout Acts and the epistles. Apparently, he came from a wealthy Jewish family, since his mother Mary, owned a large house in Jerusalem (Acts 12:12). Additionally, his cousin Barnabas, a Levite from Cyprus, also owned a large tract of land, which he sold to help support the poor (Acts 4:36–37; Colossians 4:10).

Mark traveled with Paul and Barnabas, beginning with their first missionary journey, but soon turned back for some unspecified reason (Acts 13:5, 13). This would later cause a rift between Paul and Barnabas when the latter wanted to take Mark with them on their second missionary journey, which Paul refused (Acts 15:36–41). In the end, Barnabas left with Mark, and Paul left with a man named Silas. Nevertheless, Mark's earlier vacillation would turn to strength when he matured into a fellow laborer and comfort to Paul (Colossians 4:10–11; Philemon 24). In Paul's final words, he said of Mark that he proved "useful to me for ministry" (2 Timothy 4:11). Mark would prove himself to also be a valuable asset to the apostle Peter, who affectingly referred to him as "my son" (1 Peter 5:13; ref. 1 Timothy 1:1; Titus 1:4). According to early church writers such as Papias, Justin Martyr, and others, Peter provided Mark with the material that later become the gospel that bears his name.

AUDIENCE

Mark appears to have written his gospel for a Gentile audience, perhaps those in Rome. Evidence for this comes from the fact that he: explains Jewish customs (7:3–4); translates Aramaic expressions into Greek (3:17); uses Roman reckoning of time (6:48; 13:35); and identifies Simon of Cyrene as the father of Rufus who in turn is only mentioned in the epistle to the Romans (cf. Romans 15:21; 16:13).

THEMES

Jesus is the Christ, the Son of God:
1:11; 3:11; 5:7; 8:38; 9:7; 12:6–8; 13:32; 14:36, 61; 15:39

Jesus has all authority:
1:16–34; 2:3–12, 23–28; 3:11; 4:35–41; 6:45–52; 7:1–23; 10:1–12

Jesus is God in the flesh:
3:5; 4:38; 6:6; 7:34; 8:12, 33; 10:14; 11:12; 14:33–42

Jesus, as the Christ, must suffer:
8:31; 10:45; 14:21, 36; 15:16–41

Jesus came to serve, and calls His disciples to do the same:
8:34–38; 9:35–37; 10:35–45

Jesus' gospel is for all:
1:15; 4:1–33; 9:1; 14:25; 15:43

OUTLINE

I. Jesus Prepares for Ministry (1:1–13)

II. Jesus' Ministry in Galilee and Beyond(1:14—9:29)

    a. Galilean Ministry (1:14—9:29)

        1. Calling of the disciples and Jesus' powerful deeds (1:16–45)

        2. Controversies with religious authorities (2:1—3:6)

        3. Who are Jesus' true relatives (3:7–25)

        4. Jesus teaches with parables (4:1–34)

        5. Miracles of Jesus (4:35—5:43)

        6. Rejection at Nazareth (6:1–6a)

        7. Sending out of the disciples; Death of John the Baptist (6:6b–30)

        8. Feeding the 5,000; Walking on water; Healing the sick (6:31–56)

        9. Controversies over keeping the traditions (7:1–23)

        10. More healing; Feeding the 4,000 (7:24–8:10)

        11. The Pharisees demand a sign; Warnings against the "leaven" of the Pharisees (8:11–21)

        12. Healing the blind (8:22–26)

    b. With the Disciples in Caesarea Philippi (8:27–9:29)

        1. Jesus is the Messiah; First prediction of suffering; Terms of discipleship (8:27–9:1)

        2. Transfiguration: Disciples fail to heal; Second prediction of suffering (9:2–37)

III. Jesus' Journey toward Jerusalem (9:30—10:52)

    a. Dispute over greatness; Beware of temptation 9:38–50)

    b. Teachings on: Marriage; Children as object lessons; Wealth (10:1–31)

    c. Third prediction of suffering; Another dispute over greatness (10:32–45)

    d. Healing the blind (10:46–52)

Introduction

Week 1
(Mark 1—2)

Mark does not bother with niceties to begin his story of Jesus. There is no genealogy to tell you who Jesus' great-great-great grandfather was, nor is there the familiar manger scene with baby Jesus surrounded by peaceful animals. Instead, Mark throws a glass of cold water into your face and says, "Let's go; hurry up; do I have a story to tell you!" With all the energy and excitement of a passionate storyteller, Mark will propel you through the story of Jesus at breakneck speed. All the while, Mark's goal is that you too will come to know Him as your Lord, "Jesus Christ, the Son of God" (1:1).

Mark opens his record of Jesus' life and ministry with a quick description of John the Baptist's work in preparing the way for the Lord, "Jesus Christ, the Son of God." From this starting point, Mark will sketch the beginnings of Jesus' ministry by highlighting His baptism and approval from the Father, His temptation by Satan, and His arrival in Galilee. Once in Galilee, Jesus will call His first disciples - namely Peter, Andrew, James, and John. He will begin to teach in the synagogues that the people should "repent and believe in the gospel" (1:15); and cast out unclean spirits and heal many. Word of Jesus' mighty works will then spread throughout the cities and villages of Galilee, causing crowds of people to flock to Him to hear His teachings and have their loved ones healed. As Mark continues his narrative into chapter 2, Jesus will call Levi, the tax collector to follow Him. In turn, Levi holds a feast in Jesus' honor and invites his friends who are described as "sinners." This feast then sets the stage for four conflict scenes in which Jesus clashes with the Pharisees, the religious elites of His day, over eating with "tax collectors and sinners," fasting, working on the Sabbath Day and healing on the Sabbath. These conflicts will only increase in ferocity, ultimately ending with Jesus' death on the cross.

As you read this week's text, pay special attention to—

The focus that is given to Jesus' all-encompassing authority and power:

> You will see this demonstrated by what He teaches and the way He teaches it, His ability to heal all sicknesses, expel unclean spirits, forgive sins, and interrupt religious law.

The people that Jesus called to "repent and believe in the gospel":

> He will call regular people, religious people, and even rejected people to come to Him. Jesus truly called all people to Him.

The persistence of the people who bring their loved ones to Jesus:

> Whether it's after sunset or late into the night or even if they have to take the roof off a house, people will do anything to be close to Jesus.

Week 1 ∼ Day 1

John the Baptist Prepares the Way (1:1–8)
The Baptism of Jesus (1:9–11)

*In the space below, write any observations or questions you have
regarding the text you are reading today.*

QUESTIONS

1. Describe John's role in preparing the way for Jesus' ministry?

2. In your own words, paraphrase John's description of Jesus?

3. What events occur immediately following Jesus' baptism?
   Why are these important?

4. In the first chapter of Mark, Jesus is called, "Son of God"
   (1:1), "Lord" (1:3), "Beloved Son" (1:11) and the "Holy One
   of God" (1:24). Based on these names, describe Jesus.

5. The word "gospel" means good news, so Mark is writing
   about the "good news of Jesus" (1:1). On a personal level,
   what is so good about the news of Jesus?

Week 1 ⁓ Day 2

The Temptation of Jesus (1:12–13)
Jesus Begins His Galilean Ministry (1:14–15)
Jesus Calls the First Disciples (1:16–20)

QUESTIONS

1. What twofold response does Jesus desire from those who hear His message?

2. How do Jesus' first disciples react to His call to "follow" Him?

3. Reflect on what it means to you that Jesus calls His followers to be "fishers of men"?

4. Matthew 4:1–11 provides an expanded view of Jesus' temptation. From Jesus' reactions, what lesson(s) do you take away for overcoming temptation in your life?

5. To "believe in the gospel" means more than mentally agreeing with it; rather it means to allow the gospel to change your life. In what ways will you let the gospel affect the way you live?

Week 1 ∼ Day 3

Jesus Heals a Man with an Unclean Spirit (1:21–28)
Jesus Heals Many (1:29–34)

QUESTIONS

1. Why does Jesus' teachings trigger amazement in the synagogue attendees?

2. What is the result of Jesus' teaching and miracle in the synagogue?

3. What is the immediate consequence of Jesus' fame spreading throughout the region?

4. Mark frequently uses the word "immediately" (41 times overall, 11 times in chs.1–2 alone). What do you think Mark is trying to convey about Jesus' work by using this word repeatedly?

5. Jesus is truly amazing. Whether it is His teaching (v. 27) or the miraculous displays of His power (2:12, 4:39), people are in awe of Him. What amazes you most about Jesus?

Week 1 ∽ Day 4

Jesus Preaches in Galilee (1:35–39)
Jesus Cleanses a Leper (1:40–45)
Jesus Heals a Paralytic (2:1–12)

Questions

1. How does Jesus demonstrate the importance of prayer in the life of a believer?

2. What do the leper's actions reveal about his faith in Jesus?

3. Why does Jesus forgive the paralytic's sins before He heals his body?

4. Jesus' words and actions always caused people to ask questions. Compare and contrast the question asked in 1:27 to the question in 2:6-7. How are they similar and/or different?

5. In antiquity, lepers were declared untouchable and relegated to the fringes of society, yet when Jesus heals the leper, He is "moved with pity… and touched him" (v. 41). What do you need to change in your life to follow Jesus' example of compassion for the "untouchables" of your day?

Week 1 ～ Day 5

Jesus Calls Levi (2:13–17)
A Question about Fasting (2:18–22)
Jesus is Lord of the Sabbath (2:23–28)

QUESTIONS

1. What specifically does Levi do after deciding to follow Jesus?

2. By associating with "sinners" (v. 16) is Jesus saying their sin does not matter? Explain.

3. How does Jesus answer His critics' question about why His disciples do not fast?

4. Though Jesus never commands His disciples to fast, He does anticipate they will. Using Matthew 6:16-18 as your source outline, what are Jesus' teachings for proper fasting?

5. When Levi becomes a disciple, he gives a great feast, inviting many of his friends to come and meet Jesus. Who among your friends will you invite to come and meet Jesus and learn from Him?

Week 1

Reflect ～ Respond ～ Pray

REFLECT

Mark presented Jesus as one who had all authority. His authority was displayed in what He taught and the way He taught it (1:22). It was shown in His power to perform miracles such as casting out unclean spirits and healing all manner of sickness (1:23–26, 41–42). Also, it was confirmed by His ability to forgive sins (2:5, 10–12). Finally, He even revealed His authority over all religious law by stating He was, "lord even of the Sabbath" (2:28).

1. *Since Jesus has all authority, how should you respond to Him?*

As Jesus began His ministry, He called all sorts of people to follow Him. He called regular people such as Peter, Andrew, James, and John (1:16–20). He also called religious people such as those in the synagogue at Capernaum (1:21–28). He also called rejected people like the tax collectors and sinners to repent and follow Him (2:13–17).

2. *What do the examples of Jesus calling so many different people to follow Him tell you about your own invitation to salvation?*

The story of Jesus healing the paralytic is a perfect example of the persistence that is needed in order to be in Jesus' presence. The four friends who brought the paralytic to see Jesus encountered three barriers: the large crowd, a roof, and distance (2:4). Most people would have given up, but not those men. They understood that if they were to see Jesus, they had to be persistent.

3.   *What does this story say to you about the persistence that you need in your efforts to know Jesus and to be with Him?*

Respond

In the first two chapters of Mark, you have been introduced to a Jesus who calls you to follow Him, has all authority, and is willing to forgive you of your sins. Now that you've met Jesus, what will you do today to follow Him more closely?

Pray

Use the space below to write a prayer asking God to help you respond to His authority in your life.

Introduction

Week 2
(Mark 3—4)

Following Mark's whirlwind introduction to the beginnings of Jesus' ministry, he will continue to develop his exhilarating story of Jesus and His ministry. Mark does this by highlighting Christ's movements, teachings, disciples and the growing opposition to Jesus and His work. Ultimately, the question that begs an answer is "Who is this Jesus?"

This week's reading will open with the climatic end of the conflict scenes between Jesus and the religious rulers that began in chapter 2. Specifically, the healing of the man with a withered hand will prompt the Pharisees to view Jesus as one who is to be destroyed. Because of this increased antagonism, Jesus will have to continually move His work around the Sea of Galilee teaching on the shore, in the cities and on mountains.

With Jesus' various locations serving as signposts, Mark will intertwine descriptions of the swarming crowds, with the cry of the unclean spirits who proclaim Jesus to be the "Son of God." In the midst of these two chapters, Mark tells of the calling of the twelve apostles, their inquisitiveness about the meaning of Jesus' parables, and then their fearful faithlessness during a storm. Additionally, there will be a ratcheting up of opposition to Jesus by the religious elites, who will contend that Jesus is a fraud, and by His own family, who assert He is "out of His mind."

How Mark will describe the twelve apostles:

> In this week's reading, Jesus will select twelve men whom He calls apostles. As you read about them, think through how their divergent backgrounds will aid them in their mission to preach and how even after witnessing Jesus' awe-inspiring miracles, they will be fearfully faithless in His presence.

The increased tension that occurs in the conflict scenes that Mark records in chapters 3 and 4:

> The Pharisees will be on the prowl, looking for any reason to accuse Jesus of something worthy of death or, at the very least, to discredit Him in the eyes of the people. In addition to the religious and political elites that oppose Jesus, another group of people will come on the scene in opposition to Him—His family. Pay close attention to how Jesus redefines family loyalties; it is just as shocking now as it was then.

How Jesus rewarded the apostles when they asked the reason for and the meaning of the parables:

> Jesus' use of parables will mark the dividing line between those who are just curious about Him from those who are committed to Him. For those who are committed, Jesus promises great things—if they would but pay attention to what He says.

Week 2 ∼ Day 6

A Man With A Withered Hand (3:1–6)
A Great Crowd Follows Jesus (3:7–12)

*In the space below, write any observations or questions you have
regarding the text you are reading today.*

QUESTIONS

1. What does the Pharisees' silence in response to Jesus'
    question reveal about their hearts?

2. By healing the man with the withered hand, Jesus proves it is
    lawful to do what on the Sabbath?

3. In your own words, describe the crowds that followed Jesus.

4. The Pharisees hate Jesus because He doesn't follow their
    complex rules and traditions on how to keep the Sabbath Day.
    From Exodus 20:8-11, summarize God's simple Sabbath law.

5. Despite Jesus' conflict with the religious and the political
    leaders, the crowds still flock to Him. In spite of this
    opposition would you have still followed Jesus? Why or why
    not?

Week 2 ∼ Day 7

The Twelve Apostles (3:13–21)
Blasphemy Against the Holy Spirit (3:22–30)

QUESTIONS

1. What mission does Jesus have for His twelve apostles?

2. How does Jesus' family respond to His teachings, healings, and popularity?

3. What arguments does Jesus present to prove He is not working under the power of Beelzebul?

4. In Luke 11:23, Jesus makes a soul searching declaration following His confrontation with the Pharisees. What do Jesus' words mean and in what ways could you be against Him?

5. Jesus gives three of the apostles nicknames: Simon got the name "Peter," (a stone because of his character); James and John get the name "Boanerges" or Sons of Thunder (alluding to their outspoken personalities). If Jesus were to give you a nickname, what would it be and why?

Week 2 ～ Day 8

Jesus' Mother and Brothers (3:31–35)
The Parable of the Sower (4:1–9)

1. What does Jesus mean when He states that His true family is those who do His will?

2. What teaching method does Jesus use to instruct the people?

3. List the four types of ground the Sower's seed falls on and the corresponding results.

4. While the goal of the gospel is peace with God, the immediate result may be conflict with family. From Jesus' words in Matthew 10:34–37 why should you put Him above all family ties?

5. Jesus calls those who do His will, family. What area(s) of your life do you need to change so you can be a part of Jesus' family?

Week 2 ∿ Day 9

The Purpose of Parables (4:10–20)
A Lamp Under a Basket (4:21–25)

QUESTIONS

1. In your own words, summarize Jesus' explanation of the Parable of the Sower.

2. How does the Parable of the Sower reflect people's spiritual lives?

3. What will be given to those who "pay attention" to Jesus' words?

4. What is the real difference between the disciples and those who "see but not perceive and … hear but did not understand" (v. 23)? (ref. Matthew 13:14-15)

5. From time to time in your life, your "soil type" may undergo change. Which "soil type" best represents your current spiritual life and why? What are you doing to have a "good soil" heart?

Week 2 ⁓ Day 10

The Parable of the Seed Growing (4:26–29)
The Parable of the Mustard Seed (4:30–34)
Jesus Calms a Storm (4:35–41)

QUESTIONS

1. What is the significance of the two things Jesus compares with the kingdom of God?

2. To whom does Jesus explain His parables?

3. How does Mark describe the storm and the condition of the disciple's boat?

4. There are times when it feels like God doesn't care or isn't listening. Nevertheless, what picture does Psalm 34:15–22 paint about God? What comfort do you gain from knowing God will indeed hear you when you cry out to Him?

5. No one ever spoke like Jesus (John 7:46). He amazes people, not with complex theological lectures, but with simple, down-to-earth stories. Why are Jesus' words and parables so amazing to you?

Week 2

Reflect ～ Respond ～ Pray

REFLECT

When Jesus assembled His twelve apostles He was teaching an important lesson; He can and will use the most unlikely people to accomplish His work. For example, He used four fishermen, a tax collector (a Roman sympathizer), and a Cananaean (a "Zealot" who opposed the Romans).

1. *What does this unlikely group of men tell you about Jesus' ability to use you in serving Him?*

As Jesus' popularity grew, opposition to Him came from an unlikely source, His family (3:20–21). Nevertheless, Jesus did not allow them to hinder His work. As you seek to live the life Jesus desires, you too will have family and friends who will question your intentions and abilities to be a Christian. Take a moment and reflect on who might say you are "out of your mind" for wanting to be a Christian.

2. *What arguments or reasons might they use and how will you overcome their objections?*

Jesus promises that if you "pay attention to what you hear: with the measure you use, it will be measured to you, and still more will be added to you" (4:24). In this verse, Jesus is saying that if you pay attention to His words and diligently seek to understand them, then He will reward you with blessings upon blessings of understanding and wisdom.

3. *How will knowing this promise, motivate you to continue to study His word each day?*

Respond

From the parable of the Sower, you learn that if you are going to have a "good soil" heart you have to break up compact soil, dig up rocks, and do some major weeding. What will you do today to make your heart into a "good soil" heart that is ready to receive the seed of God's word?

Pray

Use the space below to write a prayer asking God to help you respond to His word by making your heart into a "good soil" heart.

Introduction

Week 3
(Mark 5—6)

Reading about Jesus through the eyes of Mark leaves one breathless. From His constant crisscrossing of the Sea of Galilee, to His travels between the villages that surround it, to His fulfilling the needs of the multitudes that surround Him, Jesus is a man on a mission. Yet in this week's reading, you will witness a shift in Jesus' ministry, a shift from the needs of the populace to the development of His disciples. The disciples now will be the primary object of Jesus' concern as He trains them for the important role of building His church following His death, burial, and resurrection. The question is, are the disciples up to the task?

This week's reading will open with a trio of miracles that are a foretaste of the glories of Christ's Kingdom. The expelling of the demons from the demonic of the Gadarenes will give you a glimpse into a time when Satan will have no rule. With the healing of the woman with the flow of blood, Jesus will provide a glimpse into a time where there is no sickness. When Jesus gives new life to Jairus' daughter, you are previewing a kingdom where death will no longer destroy. From these three miracles, Mark will continue to move quickly through events such as: Jesus' final visit and rejection in His hometown of Nazareth, the sending of the twelve apostles out to preach, the violent death of John the Baptist, Jesus' withdrawal from Galilee for a time of rest, His miraculous feeding of the five thousand, Jesus walking on the water during a storm, and His reception in Gennesaret.

The feeling of fear that people felt in the presence of Jesus:

> Some will have their fears relieved, such as, Jairus, the woman
> with the flow of blood, or the disciples. While others such as
> the Gerasenes and the demons will continue in theirs with
> dire consequences.

How the disciples are now becoming a part of Jesus' work:

> Until now, Jesus has worked alone. He was the one
> preaching and healing; the disciples were just present in the
> background. Now, Jesus will commission them to go and
> preach, heal sickness and expel demons as well. They will also
> join Him in feeding the five thousand. From here, through
> the end of Mark, the disciples will be Jesus' primary focus
> as He prepares them for the responsibilities that lie ahead.
> However, Mark mentions something disturbing about them,
> "their hearts were hardened" (6:52). Will they prove to be the
> right people for the Jesus' mission?

How the message of repentance plays out in this week's reading:

> From the beginning of Jesus' ministry, He preached a message
> of repentance. He will continue to do so in this week's
> reading. It won't matter who the audience is, whether it's His
> hometown, or a king, or the Jews, the message is always the
> same - repent.

Week 3 ∼ Day 11

Jesus Heals a Man with a Demon (5:1–20)

*In the space below, write any observations or questions you have
regarding the text you are reading today.*

QUESTIONS

1. Give a before and after description of the man Jesus heals.

2. How do the Gerasenes react to Jesus and His great miracle?

3. Why do you think the people of the Decapolis "marveled" (v. 20) when they hear this man's story?

4. How does the demon's confession that Jesus was the "Son of the Most High God" (v. 7) underscore what James teaches in James 2:14-26 when he discusses how "faith without works is dead"?

5. Jesus wants this man to go tell those he knows best what the Lord had done for him (ref. v. 19). Name two or three friends you can share Jesus with this week.

Week 3 ～ Day 12

Jesus Heals a Woman and Jairus' Daughter (5:21–43)
Jesus Rejected at Nazareth (6:1–6)

QUESTIONS

1. In your own words, describe how you picture Jarius begging for Jesus' help.

2. How does Mark describe the woman who has the discharge of blood?

3. What do the stories of Jarius and the woman teach us about our need for faith?

4. Instead of a hero's welcome, the townspeople of Nazareth summarily reject Jesus' teachings and miracles. What additional details do you get from Luke 4:16-30 concerning this event?

5. When Jarius' servants tell him his daughter was dead, Jesus quickly replies, "Do not fear, only believe" (v. 36). How do those words speak to you today?

Week 3 ∼ Day 13

Jesus Sends Out the Twelve Apostles (6:7–13, 30–32)
The Death of John the Baptist (6:14–29)

Questions

1. What is the message the twelve proclaim as they go from city to city?

2. Why does Herod think Jesus is the resurrected John the Baptist?

3. Why does Herodias want John the Baptist killed?

4. Rather than overlooking King Herod's sin with Herodias, John is willing to confront it head on. According to Ephesians 5:11, what is the Christian's role in confronting wickedness in this world?

5. The reason that Herod gives the order for John's beheading is so he can save face in front of his guests. When has the desire to please people led you to disobey God? What will you do differently to stand firm with Jesus, regardless of the consequences?

Week 3 ∽ Day 14

Jesus Feeds the Five Thousand (6:30–44)

1. Why does Jesus want the apostles to rest a while?

2. What do you learn about Jesus from His response to the crowd?

3. Why does Jesus pray before the loaves and fishes are served? Why should you do the same?

4. Jesus is compassionate toward the people because they "were like sheep without a shepherd" (v. 34). Using the imagery of the 23rd Psalm, briefly describe how Jesus cares for His sheep.

5. In the miracle of feeding the five thousand, Jesus uses a meager five loaves and two fishes to feed a multitude. When have you seen Jesus use meager resources to meet a challenge in your life?

Week 3 ～ Day 15

Jesus Walks on the Water (6:45–52)
Jesus Heals the Sick in Gennesaret (6:53–56)

Questions

1. What lesson(s) do you learn from Jesus going up the mountain to pray?

2. What do the disciples not understand about the loaves that they should have easily recognized?

3. What is the reaction of the Gennesaret people when Jesus comes ashore?

4. Mark only records a brief summary of Jesus walking on the water. What other details does Matthew record in his account (Matthew 14:22-33)?

5. In the moment when the disciples are gripped with great fear, Jesus' words of identification, "Take heart; it is I. Do not be afraid" (v. 50) must have been reassuring. How is knowing more about Jesus helping you overcome your fears and faithlessness?

Week 3

Reflect ∿ Respond ∿ Pray

In this week's reading, you learned about a Jesus who conquers all fears. He conquered the fear of the woman with the flow of blood (5:33–34). He conquered the fears of Jarius when he thought there was no hope for his dead daughter (5:35–36). He even conquered the fears of the apostles when He walked to them on the water (5:50).

1.   *Since Jesus conquers all fears, what fears will you allow Him to conquer for you?*

Unfortunately, the miraculous feeding of the five thousand (6:30-44) didn't even faze the disciples. Even though they had participated in a miracle of truly biblical proportions, they hardened their hearts to the power of Jesus in their lives, instead of opening their hearts to Jesus (6:52). If you are not careful, you too can have a hardened heart toward the power of Jesus in your life just as they did.

2.   *How will you develop a soft heart, one that is willing to embrace Jesus and all that He offers?*

From the account of Jesus and Peter walking on the water (6:45–52; Matthew 14:22–33), a valuable lesson can be learned, "If you're going to walk on water, you have to get out of the boat." Your boat is your comfort zone. Jesus is calling for you to come to Him but you will have to leave your boat behind.

3. *What boats, (comfort zones) do you need to step out of so you can walk on the water with Jesus?*

Respond

The overall theme of Mark 5 & 6 has been letting Jesus overcome your fears and lack of faith. What will you do today to let Jesus conquer your fears and soften your heart, so you can faithfully walk with Him?

Pray

Use the space below to write a prayer asking God to help you overcome your fears.

Introduction

Week 4
(Mark 7—8)

As the gospel of Jesus steadily marches on from Galilee to Golgotha, something ironic begins to occur. The most religious people, the Pharisees, continually reject Jesus; while the outcast trust and obey Him. With a sense of foreshadowing of the makeup of the future church, Mark draws a sharp contrast between the Jewish leaders who reject Jesus, and the Gentiles who flock to Him in trusting, obedient faith. The question before you is who are you going to be most like, the Pharisees or the Gentiles, one of those who doubt or one of those who believe?

This week's reading will begin with Jesus, once again, at odds with the Pharisees and scribes over their man-made, burdensome traditions and commandments. The conflict will center on what defiles a person, a lack of external ceremonies verses the thoughts of the heart. The answer will have far-reaching implications for Mark's readers. This will then lead Jesus to move into the Gentile regions of Tyre and Sidon and then on to the Decapolis, where He heals a Gentile's daughter and a deaf man. Following these healings, the action will continue with Jesus miraculously feeding four thousand people, another dispute with the Pharisees, a misunderstanding by the disciples of Jesus' words, the unusual healing of the blind man of Bethsaida, Peter's great confession of faith, Jesus foretelling His death and resurrection, Peter's rebuke and Jesus' definition of what it means to be a true disciple. These two exciting chapters will reinforce the notion that God is pleased only with unwavering trust and faith and not with heartless rituals and traditions.

Jesus' condemnation of religious traditions:

The Pharisees will accuse Jesus' disciples of breaking the religious tradition by eating with defiled hands, which means unwashed. Their defiled, unwashed hands will have nothing to do with personal hygiene and everything to do with ritual cleanliness. In response, Jesus will tear down the Pharisees' heartless traditions that they use to circumvent God's law of love and mercy.

Jesus' warning on the dangers of believing the leaven of the Pharisees and Herod:

In the New Testament, leaven is an illustration of influence; most notably it symbolizes the evil influences of sin. The "leaven" of the Pharisees is their adherence to traditions above God's word. The "leaven" of Herod is his immoral corrupt behavior. Jesus correctly recognizes that a "little leaven, leavens the whole lump" (1 Corinthians 5:6; Galatians 5:9). As a result, He will warn the disciples against even the slightest amount of "leaven" in their lives.

What Jesus said was required for all those who would come after Him:

Jesus' portrait of a true disciple is in stark contrast to what passes for Christianity today. Jesus will teach that one must take up a cross before a crown, suffer before being glorified, and sacrifice before being rewarded. The heart of true discipleship will be that the disciple emulates his teacher in all aspects of life.

Week 4 ∼ Day 16

Traditions and Commandments (7:1–13)
What Defiles a Person (7:14-23)

*In the space below, write any observations or questions you have
regarding the text you are reading today.*

QUESTIONS

1. According to the Pharisees, what are the disciples doing wrong?

2. According to Jesus, what are the Pharisees doing wrong?

3. Do the Pharisees' "fine way" (v. 9) of doing things, remind you of any religious groups today that reject God's commands in order to keep their traditions?

4. The Pharisees practice a religion that is highly concerned with outward appearances of holiness. What radically different approach to holiness does Jesus teach in Matthew 23:25–26?

5. The attraction of traditions is that the only requirement is thoughtless conformity without a change of heart. When are you most likely to uphold religious traditions rather than honor God with your whole heart?

Week 4 ～ Day 17

The Syrophoenician Woman's Faith (7:24–30)
Jesus Heals a Deaf Man (7:31–37)

QUESTIONS

1. What geographical region does Jesus withdraw to in order to have some solitude?

2. Why does Jesus finally respond to the woman, following what seems to be an indifferent attitude?

3. Detail the unusual way Jesus heals the man who is deaf and mute.

4. Using Matthew 15:23 as your source, contrast the disciples' attitude toward the Syrophoenician woman and Jesus' attitude. What troubling qualities do you see in the disciples?

5. The way Jesus talks to the Syrophoenician woman offends our modern sensibilities, however, put yourself in her place for a moment. What would you have done if you desperately needed Jesus and He talked to you that way? Explain your answer.

Week 4 ~ Day 18

Jesus Feeds the Four Thousand (8:1–10)
The Pharisees Demand a Sign (8:11–12)
The Leaven of the Pharisees and Herod (8:13–21)

QUESTIONS

1. Describe the great crowd that Jesus feeds with the seven loafs and few fishes.

2. Why does Jesus "sigh deeply in His spirit" (v. 12) when the Pharisees ask for a sign from heaven?

3. In light of all the disciples hear and witnesses, why do they not fully understand Jesus?

4. In an earlier scene (Matthew 12:38–42) Jesus says the only "sign" the Pharisees will receive is the sign of Jonah. What is the "sign of Jonah" and how does it prove Jesus to be the Christ?

5. One thing is for sure, the disciples are not thinking about Jesus' greatness as they gather up the multiple baskets of leftovers after He feeds thousands with a few loaves and fishes. Name two or three things you will do to become more aware of the awesome blessings Jesus has given you.

Week 4 ～ Day 19

Jesus Heals a Blind Man at Bethsaida (8:22-26)
Peter Confesses Jesus as the Christ (8:27-30)

QUESTIONS

1. Describe Jesus' healing of the blind man at Bethsaida.

2. How do you think this healing relates back to the discussion in the boat?

3. Why do you think Jesus does not want the blind man or the disciples to go public about Him?

4. What additional insights do you get from Peter's confession of Jesus as the Christ from the parallel accounts of Matthew 16:13-20 and Luke 9:18-20?

5. Many people today say that Jesus was a good moral teacher, or a great philosopher, or a noteworthy historical figure, or literary myth, but who do you say that He is? Why?

Week 4 ∽ Day 20

Jesus Foretells His Death and Resurrection (8:31—9:1)

QUESTIONS

1. How does Jesus define Himself as the suffering Savior?

2. Why does Jesus require a person to "deny himself" (v. 34) before they can follow Him?

3. "What does it profit a man if he gained the whole world and forfeited his soul?" (v. 36)

4. Jesus' demand for you to deny yourself and to take up your cross is a call for you to model your life after His. According to Philippians 2:5-8, how did Jesus deny Himself for you?

5. In our do-whatever-feels-good society, Jesus' demands of discipleship are challenging to say the least. What goes through your mind when you think about sacrificing your desires to conform to Jesus' will for you and your life?

Week 4

Reflect ∾ Respond ∾ Pray

Because Jesus didn't observe the religious commandments of men He was in constant conflict with the Pharisees. The lesson from Jesus' teaching on traditions is that if you teach and practice the commandments and traditions of men as being on par with or rather than the commandments of God, then your worship of God is hypocritical and in vain (Mark 7:1-13).

1. *What are some of the commandments and traditions of men that might invalidate our devotion to God?*

In Jesus' warning to His disciples, "Watch out; beware of the leaven of the Pharisees and the leaven of Herod" (Mark 8:15), you learned that the disciples were to: Watch out for and not practice the self-righteous religions of the Pharisees (7:1-23, Matthew 16:12), and watch out for and not mimic the immoral conduct of Herod (6:14-29) because "a little leaven leavens the whole lump" (ref. 1 Corinthians 5:6; 15:33; Galatians 5:9).

2. *Why is it especially important that you beware of practicing self-righteous religion and/or practice even a slightest immorality of the world around you?*

In Jesus' instructions to those who would follow Him, He taught this eternal truth: when He comes in glory, He will be ashamed of those who were ashamed of Him and His words (8:38).

3. *What did Jesus mean by this statement? List some steps you need to take to stand up for Jesus and His gospel.*

Respond

In this week's reading you learned that if you are going to be Jesus' disciple, then you have to deny yourself, take up your cross, and follow Him (7:34). What will you do today to live out this truth?

Pray

Use the space below to write a prayer asking God to help you to do whatever it takes to live a sacrificial life for Him.

Introduction

Week 5
(Mark 9—10)

In Mark's usual action-packed style of writing, he moves through the events of chapters 9—10 at a fast clip, constantly driving the reader to the climax of Jesus' death, burial, and resurrection. On the surface, the events and teachings in these two chapters don't seem connected, however, Jesus is deliberately moving in the direction of Jerusalem. All the while equipping His disciples for their role as the foundation of His church. The question the disciples must answer is, if Jesus is the Christ, why does He keep talking about His death in Jerusalem?

In the short span of 102 verses, Mark will quickly move through saturated passages on Jesus' transfiguration, an explanation of Elijah's role in the Messiah's kingdom, Jesus' healing of a boy with an unclean spirit; again, Jesus foretells His coming death, burial and resurrection, the disciples argue over who is the greatest among them, and Jesus defines the Kingdom of Greatness. Furthermore, Mark transitions from Jesus' Galilean ministry to His last week in Jerusalem. While traveling toward His death, Mark will tell of Jesus' confrontation with the Pharisees over marriage and divorce; how He welcomes and blesses children; His encounter with a rich young man; His third foretelling to the disciples of His upcoming death; how Christ once again squelches the disciples' taste for glory; and His healing of blind Bartimaeus. A careful study of these chapters will reveal Jesus' efforts to equip the disciples with an important number of Kingdom truths.

Jesus' definition of kingdom greatness:

The disciples were concerned with one thing—being the greatest disciple of Jesus. In their minds, the road to greatness was paved with power and prestige. Yet, Jesus will challenge their definition of greatness with a radically different answer than the disciples were expecting. In Jesus' kingdom, He will turn the leadership pyramid on its head. In the process of defining what it means to be great, Jesus will detail His own purpose and the purpose of everyone who follows Him.

The hyperbolic way Jesus demands extreme measures to avoid sin:

From the beginning of His ministry, Jesus taught that people should repent of their sins. However, He does not stop there; not only are believers supposed to repent after they sin, but they are to avoid sinning at any cost. As a means to motivate believers to disconnect from temptations that cause them to sin, Jesus will point to the horrors of hell that awaits all who indulge in sinful lifestyles.

How Jesus turns to the creation account in Genesis as the foundation for His teaching on the permanency of marriage:

Jesus' application of the creation account will not only challenge the Pharisees and the disciples' view of marriage, but it will also confront modern views of marriage and divine creation as well.

Week 5 — Day 21

The Transfiguration (9:2–13)
Jesus Heals A Boy with an Unclean Spirit (9:14–29)

In the space below, write any observations or questions you have regarding the text you are reading today.

Questions

1. Describe Jesus' transfigured appearance.

2. What motivates Peter to speak while Jesus converses with Elijah and Moses?

3. What do you think Jesus means by, "This kind only comes out with prayer and fasting" (v. 29 NKJV)?

4. Many years later Peter and John (2 Peter 1:16–19; John 1:14) described what they saw when Jesus was transfigured. Why do you think they remind their readers of this event?

5. Everyone struggles with his or her faith from time to time. In what ways does the father's plea, "I believe, help my unbelief" (v. 24) echo your own prayers?

Week 5 ∾ Day 22

Jesus Again Foretells His Death and Resurrection (9:30–32)
Who is the Greatest? (9:33–37)
Anyone Not Against Us Is for Us (9:38–41)

Questions

1. Why do the disciples not understand the plain meaning of
    Jesus' teaching on His death?

2. What does the disciples' discussion on the road to
    Capernaum reveal about their hearts?

3. How does Jesus' attitude toward the unnamed exorcist differ
    from John's?

4. Jesus says those who would be first in His kingdom must
    be, "last of all and servant to all" (v. 35). From Philippians
    2:3-4, what do you learn is the essence of Jesus' command of
    servanthood?

5. Serving others by putting their interests before your own goes
    against society's philosophy of looking out for "numero uno."
    Why is Jesus' teaching of service sometimes hard to swallow?

Week 5 ∽ Day 23

Temptations to Sin (9:42–50)
Teaching about Divorce (10:1–12)

Questions

1. What does Jesus say would be "better" (v. 42) for a person than to cause a believer to sin? Explain.

2. In your own words, explain Jesus' teaching on how to avoid sin.

3. Why is the Pharisees' question about divorce a test for Jesus?

4. Read the original marriage passages of Genesis 1:26-28, 2:18-25: What reasons do you find for understanding marriage to be the permanent union between one man and one woman?

5. Jesus expects His disciples to take radical measures to avoid sin. What are some things in your life that you need to cut off and tear out because they are leading you into sin?

Week 5 ～ Day 24

Let the Children Come to Me (10:13–16)
The Rich Young Man (10:17–31)

QUESTIONS

1. How does one receive the Kingdom like a child?

2. Describe the Rich Young Man (ref. Matthew 19:16–29; Luke 18:18–30).

3. In what concrete ways are those who have left all for Jesus rewarded in this life and the next?

4. In this week's reading, Jesus uses children as object lessons on two different occasions (9:33–37, 42; 10:13–16). What truths about salvation do you glean from these interactions?

5. Does maintaining or improving your material lifestyle get in the way of following Jesus? If so, how and what steps will you take to give your life to Christ, not stuff?

Week 5 ∼ Day 25

Jesus Foretells His Death a Third Time (10:32–34)
The Request of James and John (10:35–45)
Jesus Heals Blind Bartimaeus (10:46–52)

QUESTIONS

1. What events does Jesus say will occur to Him in Jerusalem?

2. How does Jesus react to James and John's request and the other ten disciples' anger?

3. Summarize the story of Jesus healing blind Bartimaeus.

4. Contrast the two answers to Jesus' question, "What do you want Me to do for you?" (vv. 36, 51). How does the nature of James and John's request (v. 37), differ from Bartimaeus' (v. 51)?

5. What is your answer to Jesus' question, "What do you want Me to do for you?"

Week 5

Reflect ∼ Respond ∼ Pray

REFLECT

Following James and John's bold request for honor and power, Jesus taught them, and the rest of the disciples, that true glory comes from serving others. As proof, He offered Himself as an example saying, "For even the Son of Man came not to be served but to serve and to give His life as a ransom for many" (10:45). The theme of Jesus ransoming Christians is discussed in 1 Corinthians 6:19–20; Titus 2:15;1 Peter 1:17–19.

1. *Describe what it means to you that Jesus came "not to be served" but to give His life a "ransom for many".*

In a very highly illustrative way, Jesus expressed His expectation that His followers should do whatever it takes to avoid sin (9:43–48).

2. *Why do you think Jesus wants you to avoid sinning at all costs?*

By Jesus establishing His teaching of marriage and divorce on the creation account (10:6–8), He confirmed the validity of the creation as it is recorded in Genesis 1—3. While a faith in a literal, six-day creation runs counter to modern scientific thinking, God calls Christians to understand the creation by the means of faith and not scientific reasoning (ref. Hebrews 11:3). Many spiritual truths are dependent upon an understanding that "the universe was created by the word of God." (ref. John 1:1-3; Romans 5:12–21; Acts 4:23–31; Acts 14:8–18; and 1 Timothy 2:11–15)

3. *Using the above passages, what truths are established on the fact that God did indeed create the heavens and the earth?*

Respond

In this week's reading, you learned that Jesus wants us to take extreme measures to keep from sinning. What extreme measures are you going to take today to keep from sinning?

Pray

Use the space below to write a prayer asking God to help you take extreme measures to avoid sin at all cost.

Introduction

Week 6
(Mark 11—12)

Pushing you ever closer toward the climatic conclusion of Jesus' ministry, Mark records the most significant royal reception in history, the ceremonial entry of Jesus into Jerusalem. However, this is no ordinary entrance, because this is no ordinary king; His kingdom is like none before or since. Jesus' arrival causes quite a stir, not only for the reception He receives, but also for His final actions and teachings as He marches on to the cross. The question is, how long will the goodwill of Jesus' reception last before the religious leaders try to destroy Him?

In a fashion fit for a king, Jesus will enter Jerusalem to the shouts of the people and the disdain of the religious officials. On the following day, He will cause an even greater public stir by forcibly driving merchants from the temple by chasing their animals away and overturning their tables. To underscore His judgment of the hypocritical nature of the Jews' worship, Mark will artfully bracket the temple scene with Jesus cursing a barren fig tree. When the disciples ask about the tree, Jesus will take the opportunity to teach on the necessity of faith and forgiveness in prayer. As if on cue, the religious leaders will come to Jesus demanding to know the source of His authority. However, Jesus will skillfully put them on the defensive with a probing question and a scathing parable. Following this encounter, other religious leaders will attempt to discredit Jesus by posing a tricky, political question and a complicated, theological conundrum. As always, Jesus' brilliant responses will silence His critics. Not to be outdone, Jesus will then turn the tables on the Pharisees and begin to ask them a question or two. Mark 12 will conclude with a sincere scribe approaching Jesus with a question, a warning from Jesus about religious hypocrisy, and then a lesson on giving.

AS YOU READ THIS WEEK'S TEXT, PAY SPECIAL ATTENTION TO—

Jesus' teaching on the necessity of faith and forgiveness as a component to having your prayers heard and answered:

Using a withered fig tree as an object lesson, Jesus will teach the disciples that the kinds of prayers that move mountains are rooted in faith and forgiveness. While the first ingredient is understandable, the latter is nonetheless challenging.

Jesus' rebuke of the chief priest and scribes through the telling of the scathing Parable of the Tenants and the quoting of Psalm 118:22–23:

Both the parable and the quotation from Psalms will reveal that something new is on the horizon to replace the old temple and its hypocritical leaders. Unlike previous parables and teachings, the Parable of the Tenants needs no explanation, the chief priests will know instantly that Jesus has targeted them and their hatred of Him will greatly intensify.

Jesus' response to a sincere scribe:

A scribe will come along and endorse Jesus' answer that to love God and one's neighbor was greater than all temple offerings and sacrifices. By stating that the scribe was "not far from the kingdom," Jesus will be emphasizing that the scribe was not yet in the kingdom. This is a challenge to the scribe, and to you, to move beyond sincere agreement with Jesus' teachings and to totally submit to His authority.

Week 6 ～ Day 26

The Triumphal Entry (11:1–11)

In the space below, write any observations or questions you have regarding the text you are reading today.

QUESTIONS

1. Why do you think Jesus instructs His disciples to retrieve a colt for Him in such an unusual way?

2. What details of Jesus' celebratory entry into Jerusalem stand out most to you?

3. Why does Jesus shift from avoiding public attention early on, to now receiving much praise?

4. Jesus uses Psalm 118 twice in this week's reading (vv. 9–10; 12:10–11). What familiar verses do you notice in this Psalm and how does it enhance the scenes of Mark 11—12?

5. Only kings are welcomed with choruses of praise and clothes spread out on the road. How does Jesus' kingship call for you to praise Him with your voice and possessions?

Week 6 ∼ Day 27

Jesus Curses the Fig Tree (11:12–14)
Jesus Cleanses the Temple (11:15–19)
The Lesson of the Withered Fig Tree (11:20–25)

QUESTIONS

1. What does Jesus' cursing of the fig tree represent?

2. How different are the temple and its worship from what Jesus says it is supposed to be?

3. Summarize Jesus' teaching on faith and prayer. (ref. Matthew 6:9-15; Luke 11:1-4)

4. How do John 15:7 and James 4:3 further clarify Jesus' promises of answered prayers?

5. According to 1 Corinthians 6:19, your body is to be a temple of the Holy Spirit. Is your temple a house of prayer or a den of robbers? What tables does Jesus need to overturn and what moneychangers does He need to drive out of your heart so that you can be a holy temple for God?

Week 6 ～ Day 28

The Authority of Jesus Challenged (11:27–33)
The Parable of the Tenants (12:1–12)
Paying Taxes to Caesar (12:13–17)

QUESTIONS

1. What motivates the Jewish leaders to continue to plot Jesus' demise?

2. What is the meaning of the Parable of the Tenants?

3. The Pharisees and Herodians' question about taxes is an attempt to get Jesus to say or do what?

4. What insights do Matthew 3:1–12 and Luke 3:1–20 give you regarding John's relationship with the people and the leaders of Jerusalem and Judea?

5. Since Caesar's money bears his image, Jesus says, "Render to Caesar the things that are Caesar's" (v. 17). Therefore, since you bear God's image (Genesis 1:26–27), you are to, "[Render] to God the things that are God's." Specifically, what do you need to render to God?

Week 6 ∼ Day 29

The Sadducees Ask About the Resurrection? (12:18–27)
The Great Commandment (12:28–34)
Whose Son Is the Christ (12:35–37)

1. How does Jesus turn the Sadducees' trick question around to
    point out their own folly?

2. Describe what it means to "love God with all your heart …
    and your neighbor as yourself" (vv. 30–31).

3. Contrast how Jesus responds to the sincere scribe and the
    hypocritical Pharisees.

4. Read Matthew 22:41–46 for more details concerning Jesus'
    question, "Whose Son is the Christ?". How does Jesus turn
    the tables on the Pharisees with this one question?

5. The greatest command of all scripture is to love God with all
    your heart, soul, mind, and strength. What do you need to
    change in your life, so that you can love God with your all?

Week 6 ～ Day 30

Beware of the Scribes (12:38–40)
The Widow's Offering (12:41–44)

QUESTIONS

1. Why does Jesus want His disciples to beware of the scribes?

2. Why does Jesus consider the poor widow's offering to be more than that of the rich?

3. What lesson(s) do you think Jesus wants the disciples to learn from the example of the widow?

4. The Jewish religious establishment hates Jesus because He exposed their hypocrisy. Using Matthew 23:1–36, summarize Jesus' seven woes against the scribes and Pharisees.

5. At the heart of sacrificial giving is a trust that God will provide any need. Has a lack of trust kept you from sacrificially giving? If so, what will you do to cultivate more trust in God?

Week 6

Reflect ∽ Respond ∽ Pray

REFLECT

In Jesus' teaching on prayer (Mark 11:22–26), He taught that forgiving others is the basis for having your prayers heard and having your own sins forgiven (ref. Matthew 6:14–15; 18:23–34; Colossians 3:12–14).

1. *Why do you think Jesus would place such emphasis on forgiving others?*

As Jesus concludes the Parable of the Tenants, He quotes Psalm 118:22–23, the same psalm the people shouted as Jesus entered Jerusalem. Jesus is the rejected son in the parable who now becomes the rejected cornerstone of a great building. The great building is the church, the new temple in which God now dwells, built upon Jesus (Acts 4:10–12; Ephesians 2:19–22; 1 Peter 2:2-8).

2. *How does this affect the way you view the church (not a building, but saved people) and its role in your life?*

While the sincere scribe approved of Jesus' teaching, and even commended His answer, Jesus said he was "not far from the kingdom of God;" meaning he was not yet in the kingdom. To be in the kingdom one must do more than approve of Jesus' teachings; one must submit entirely to Him and His teachings. (ref. James 2:14–26)

3.   *Why is it not enough to merely agree with Jesus' teachings?*

RESPOND

In this week's reading, you learned that God wants all your heart, soul, mind and strength because He created you in His image. What will you do this week to remove any barriers that are keeping you from giving all your love to God?

PRAY

Use the space below to write a prayer asking God to help you respond to His word by giving Him all your love.

Introduction

Week 7
(Mark 13—14)

In the efficiently fast style of Mark, the events of Jesus' last week are delivered with even more rapid fire than before. Jesus enters Jerusalem with shouts of gladness from the people but to anger and fury from the Jewish religious leaders. Because of His cleansing of the temple and His denouncement of the scribes and Pharisees, Jesus is on a fast track to the cross. Those who seek to take Jesus' life will stop at nothing to destroy Him. While those who follow Him will do everything to worship Him and express their extreme loyalty to Him but, in the end they will desert Him. The question is, what will you do?

This week's reading is filled with both drama and emotion. It begins with what is commonly called the Olivet Discourse, since Jesus delivered this sermon on Mt. Olivet, east of the temple. In His sermon, Jesus will explain to the disciples the signs that would occur prior to the destruction of the temple that stands before them. He will repeatedly warn them to "be on guard" as they watched for the signs that His judgment was about to come upon Jerusalem and the hypocritical Jewish religious leaders. As the last day of Jesus' life opens in Mark 14, Jesus, to the disdain of the disciples, will allow a woman to anoint him with a very costly ointment; Judas will then agree to betray Jesus; Jesus and the disciples will celebrate the Passover together, during which, Jesus will institute the Lord's Supper. In the same night, while praying in the Garden of Gethsemane, Jesus will be arrested by a mob of soldiers led by Judas, the disciples will flee, Jesus will be put on trial and condemned to death, and, just as Jesus had predicted, Peter will deny Him three times.

The question Jesus is answering with His discourse on the destruction of the temple:

Mark 13 is an often abused passage by the false teachers of premillennialism. Jesus will be focused on the destruction of Jerusalem and the temple. Note the times that Jesus tells His disciples to "be on guard" (13:9, 23, 33), the specific nature of the Jews role in the tribulation, and where Jesus tells his followers to flee when they know the time for destruction is upon them. When viewed in context, Mark 13 is an easy to understand passage that answers more questions than it raises.

Jesus' prayers in the Garden of Gethsemane:

Alone in the garden, Jesus will pour out His heart and soul to the Father, asking that the hour of His death might pass from Him. Though His soul is very sorrowful, almost to the point of death, with His face to the ground Jesus will pray not for His will, but for God's will to be done. Through Jesus' prayers in the garden, you will see both His humanity and His willingness to do the Father's will, converge.

Judas' betrayal:

Judas is a name that evokes devilish images of betrayal to the highest degree. In the final day of Jesus' life, Judas will come to the forefront, not as a loyal disciple but as an evil betrayer. He will betray Jesus, not for lofty ideological reasons, rather, for the basest of reasons—money. The story of Judas is one that should shock you into examining your own walk with Jesus, because you can be more like Judas than you would think.

Week 7 ～ Day 31

Jesus Teaches on the Coming Destruction of Jerusalem
(13:1–37)

*In the space below, write any observations or questions you have
regarding the text you are reading today.*

QUESTIONS

1. What event do some of the disciples privately question Jesus about?

2. What phrases show that Jesus' focus is on the destruction of the temple before Him?

3. How does Jesus want His disciples to act as they live through the tribulation?

4. Jesus draws on Old Testament language to signify the world-changing nature of the events He was describing. What similar language is used to describe the destruction of the Babylonians (Isaiah 13:10), Egyptians (Isaiah 19:1; Ezekiel 32:7) and the Ninevites (Nahum 1:1–3)?

5. Much of the writing on end-times prophecies essentially reduces the bible to an end-times horoscope of sorts. However, what does this passage teach you about leaving such issues to God and trusting Him as you await Jesus' final return?

Week 7 ∼ Day 32

The Plot to Kill Jesus (14:1–2)
Jesus Anointed at Bethany (14:3–9)
Judas to Betray Jesus (14:10–11)

QUESTIONS

1. Why do the chief priest and scribes not want to arrest and kill Jesus during the Passover?

2. Why is it difficult for some of the disciples to see the value of the woman's anointing of Jesus?

3. How does the woman's action contrast with those of the chief priest and Judas?

4. Read Matthew 26:6–13 and John 12:1–8. What additional details do you get regarding the woman's identity, how she administers her gift and the individuals who scolded her?

5. At three hundred denarii, the alabaster flask of ointment represents nearly a year's worth of wages for the average laborer (ref. Matthew 20:2). How does the story of Mary's costly act of love, and Jesus' response, motivate you to serve Him? In what ways will you emulate her example?

Week 7 ∼ Day 33

The Passover with the Disciples (14:12–21)
Institution of the Lord's Supper (14:22–25)
Jesus Foretells Peter's Denial (14:26–31)

QUESTIONS

1. What do the two disciples do to prepare for the Passover?

2. What new meaning does Jesus give to the bread and the fruit of the vine?

3. What are you to conclude about Jesus from His ability to know how events will transpire?

4. Following the pattern of the early church (ref. Acts 20:7), we partake of the Lord's Supper every Sunday. What benefit(s) do you think there is to taking the Lord's Supper every first day of the week?

5. "Pride goes before destruction, a haughty spirit before a fall" (Proverbs 16:18) echoes in the background of Peter and the disciples' claim they will never desert Jesus. Think of a time when your pride led you to make a bold claim you did not keep. What were the disastrous results?

Week 7 ∼ Day 34

Jesus Prays in Gethsemane (14:32–42)
Betrayal and Arrest of Jesus (14:43–50)
A Young Man Flees (14:51–52)

QUESTIONS

1. Describe Jesus' prayers in the garden.

2. What do you learn about Jesus from the way He allows His emotions to shape His prayers?

3. What does Jesus suggest will be the result of the disciples' failure to watch and pray?

4. From Luke 22:47–53 and John 18:1–11, what additional details surrounding Jesus' arrest jump out at you?

5. There's no doubt the disciples could tell Jesus was deeply distressed. However, rather than praying, the disciples slept. Why is prayer often so difficult even when you have the best of intentions?

Week 7 ∼ Day 35

Jesus Faces the Council (14:53–65)
Peter Denies Jesus (14:66–72)

QUESTIONS

1. What testimony causes the council to decide to condemn Jesus to death?

2. How does Peter's failure to stay awake and pray affect his ability to resist temptation?

3. Contrast Jesus' response during His trial to Peter's responses to the servants/bystanders' inquiries.

4. In response to the High Priest's question, "Are you the Christ, the Son of the Blessed?" (v. 61), Jesus references Psalm 110 and Daniel 7:13–14. What do these two passages reveal about Jesus?

5. Peter says he will follow Jesus to the death; he even fights for Jesus, yet in the end, Peter flees and three times he denies knowing Jesus (14:31, 47, 50, 66–72). How does knowing about Peter's sin and later repentance help you see that all is not lost when you succumb to temptation?

Week 7

Reflect ∽ Respond ∽ Pray

REFLECT

The scene of persecution and judgment that Jesus described in Mark 13 is dark and brooding. Yet, cast against this scene of judgment and recompense, Jesus gave the disciples hope of their salvation. The destruction of Jerusalem would be God's judgment against a wicked people who rejected their Messiah and persecuted His messengers.

1. *What images come to mind when you read Mark 13? In what way(s), does the faithful rising above the judgment encourage you to stay true to the Lord?*

In the garden, Jesus prayed, "Abba, Father, all things are possible for You. Remove this cup from Me. Yet not what I will, but what You will" (v. 36). Jesus' prayer in Gethsemane teaches that while God desires to hear your petitions and has all power to bring about your desires, ultimately you must submit your life to His will, not your own.

2. *Describe the kind of faith and trust you need to have to fully submit your life to God's will.*

In this week's reading, the actions of Judas (scolding Mary, 14:4-5; John 12:4-6) over the expensive fragrance and betraying Jesus for money (14:10-11) confirmed the truth of 1 Timothy 6:10, "The love of money is a root of all kinds of evils."

3.   *Why is it that the love of money causes people to commit all sorts of evil? What can you do to keep yourself from sinning because of money?*

From the account of Peter denying Jesus, you learned the value of not thinking too highly of yourself because the "spirit indeed is willing, but the flesh is weak" (14:38b). What will you do this week to practice Jesus' remedy of watching and praying "so that you will not enter into temptation" (14:38a)?

Use the space below to write a prayer asking God to help you respond to His word to watch and pray.

Introduction

Week 8
(Mark 15 — 16)

From the beginning of Mark's gospel, he has propelled you through the story of Jesus with the excitement of a passionate storyteller, coupled with the speed of a race car driver, just so he could tell you how the story ends. The death of Jesus on the cross is the focal point of God's plan of redemption. It serves as the ultimate demonstration of love by a good and gracious God. Yet, the story of Jesus does not end with the cross; rather, it ends with an empty tomb. Over the course of the last two millennia, the story of Jesus' crucifixion and His glorious resurrection has stood as the greatest story ever told, not because of its gripping storyline, rather, because these two events provide the believer salvation and hope through Jesus Christ. Again, the ultimate purpose of Mark's gospel echoes from beginning to end, this is "Jesus Christ, the Son of God" (1:1). Will you believe in Him and be baptized?

Mark will dedicate forty-seven verses to chronicle the last few hours of Jesus' life. Beginning with Jesus' trial before Pilate, Mark will quickly tell of the people's choice of the infamous murderer Barabbas over Jesus, then Jesus' mocking and beating at the hands of Roman soldiers, His crucifixion and death on the cross, followed by His burial in another man's tomb. Mark 16 will pick up the story three days after His death. On the first day of the week, a group of women will arrive at Jesus' borrowed tomb to find His body gone and an angel who proclaims He has risen from the dead. Mark's gospel will end with a postscript of sorts that entails a brief collection of Jesus' post-resurrection appearance, and the Lord's own words on how a person is saved, and a synopsis of the apostles' actions, "And they went out and preached everywhere, while the Lord worked with them and confirmed the message by accompanying signs" (16:20).

How Jesus' death on the cross fulfilled, not only Jesus' own prophecies, but many Old Testament prophecies as well: The death of Jesus on the cross was no accident; rather, it has been a part of God's eternal plan from the beginning of time to save humanity through the death of Jesus, the Lamb of God.

The resurrection of Jesus and the central role it plays in Christian teaching:

The resurrection of Jesus is the foundation of the Christian faith. Without a resurrected Jesus, there is no faith, there is no salvation, and there is no hope of eternity with Him in heaven.

The instructions that Jesus gives to the apostles before He ascends into heaven:

Commonly known as the Great Commission, Jesus will spell out for His apostles their mission and how a person is saved. Unfortunately, many in the religious world have rejected even Jesus' own words.

Week 8 ∽ Day 36

Jesus Faces Pilate (15:1–5)
Pilate Delivers Jesus to Be Crucified (15:6–15)

In the space below, write any observations or questions you have regarding the text you are reading today.

QUESTIONS

1. How does Jesus react to the chief priest's many accusations?

2. Why does Pilate allow Jesus' execution to proceed even though he knows Jesus is innocent?

3. In your own words, describe Barabbas.

4. In His trial before Pilate, Jesus acknowledges that He is the rightful king of Israel. From the parallel passage of John 18:34–37, how does Jesus describe the nature of His kingdom?

5. In a way, Barabbas represents every human who has ever lived, a sinner of the highest degree (ref. Romans 3:23). Just as the crowd chooses Barabbas over Jesus, God chooses you to live and His son to die in your place. How will you let God's demonstration of love for you change your life?

Week 8 ∽ Day 37

Jesus is Mocked (15:16–20)
The Crucifixion (15:21–32)

QUESTIONS

1. Describe the various ways the Roman soldiers mock Jesus.

2. What detail(s) from Mark's brief account of Jesus' crucifixion stands out most to you?

3. What is ironic about the contemptuous statements directed at Jesus as He hangs on the cross?

4. Mark's account of Jesus' crucifixion is short on specifics concerning His death. What insight does Isaiah 53:1–12 provide concerning the spiritual details of Jesus' agonizing death on the cross?

5. All that Jesus suffered, (the scourging, mocking, beating, and the cross) He suffered for you. As you see Jesus on the cross and all that He endured, what emotions come to the surface?

Week 8 ～ Day 38

The Death of Jesus (15:33-41)
Jesus Is Buried (15:42-47)

QUESTIONS

1. What convinces the centurion that Jesus is the "Son of God" (v. 39)?

2. Who makes up the group of people who looked "on from a distance" (v. 40–41) while Jesus died?

3. Who is Joseph of Arimathea and why does he request Jesus' body? (see also: John 19:38–42)

4. By quoting Psalm 22:1 from the cross, Jesus evokes the whole of the Psalm as pertaining to Himself. Compare Mark 15:16–39 to Psalm 22:1–18. What parallels do you find between the two passages?

5. By asking for Jesus' body, Joseph of Arimathea risks losing his position, power and prestige. Nevertheless, "he took courage," (v. 43) and publicly showed his love for Jesus. Name one thing you need to publicly do for Jesus. What steps will you take to "take courage" and do it?

Week 8 ∽ Day 39

The Resurrection (16:1–8)
Jesus Appears to Mary Magdalene (16:9–11)
Jesus Appears to Two Disciples (16:12–13)

QUESTIONS

1. What do the women expect to find when they go to the tomb?

2. Describe what the women see and hear at the tomb.

3. Why do you think the disciples do not believe the reports that Jesus had risen from the dead?

4. Jesus' resurrection is one of the central truths of Christianity. According to Acts 17:31; Romans 1:4; 8:34; and 1 Corinthians 15:17, what does the resurrection of Jesus prove?

5. Are there times when, like the women at the tomb, fear keeps you from telling others the good news of Jesus. Why were you afraid? Obviously, they overcame their fears, so how will you develop more courage to overcome yours?

Week 8 ∼ Day 40

The Great Commission (16:14–20)

QUESTIONS

1. What does Jesus do when He appears to the eleven disciples?

2. According to Jesus, who can be saved?

3. Why do the early believers need the signs listed in vv. 17–18? (ref. Romans 15:18–19; Hebrews 2:2–4)

4. From Jesus' final words, you learn the importance of baptism in the life of the believer. How do such passages as Acts 2:37–38; 22:16; Romans 6:3–11; 1 Peter 3:18–22 picture baptism as how a believer unites themselves to Christ and is saved?

5. Take a moment and reflect on your study of Mark. How has your understanding of Jesus and His mission grown? How has your study of Mark strengthened your faith?

Week 8

Reflect ∼ Respond ∼ Pray

REFLECT

The death of Jesus on the cross was no accident; rather, it was part of God's eternal plan from the beginning of time to save humanity through the death of His Son. (ref. Acts 2:23; Isaiah 53:5–12; John 1:29; 1 Peter 1:20–21)

1. *Using the above passages, what do you learn about the importance of Jesus' death on the cross for you?*

The resurrection of Jesus on the first day of the week was proof that He will judge the world in the final day (Acts 17:30–31), that He was the Son of God (Romans 1:4), and that the resurrection provides substance to our faith (1 Corinthians 15:13–22).

2. *What difference then, does the resurrection make in how you live your life?*

From Jesus' Great Commission (Mark 16:14–20; Matthew 28:16–20), you learned that to be His disciple you must believe, be baptized, and keep His commandments.

3.   *What is the significance of these three marks of discipleship?*

RESPOND

In this week's reading, you learned that everyone who believes in Jesus, is baptized, and keeps His commandments will be saved. What do you need to do today (or keep doing) in order to be saved?

PRAY

Use the space below to write a prayer asking God to help you respond to His promise of salvation.